50 Speedy Supper Recipes

By: Kelly Johnson

Table of Contents

- Quick Stir-Fry Beef and Veggies
- 15-Minute Garlic Shrimp Pasta
- Easy One-Pan Chicken Fajitas
- Spicy Veggie Tacos
- One-Pot Garlic Parmesan Pasta
- Chicken Caesar Salad Wraps
- Quick Veggie and Bean Chili
- 20-Minute Chicken Alfredo
- Easy Beef Stir-Fry with Broccoli
- Quick Teriyaki Chicken Skewers
- One-Pot Beef Stroganoff
- Garlic Butter Shrimp and Asparagus
- 15-Minute Veggie Fried Rice
- Quick BBQ Chicken Quesadillas
- 30-Minute Salmon and Veggie Packets
- One-Skillet Lemon Herb Chicken
- Fast Chicken Parmesan

- 20-Minute Fish Tacos
- Spaghetti Aglio e Olio
- One-Pot Spaghetti Bolognese
- Veggie and Hummus Pita Pockets
- Grilled Cheese and Tomato Soup
- 30-Minute Beef and Broccoli
- Quick Sweet and Sour Chicken
- Sheet Pan Chicken and Veggies
- Quick Baked Ziti
- Teriyaki Beef Bowls
- 15-Minute Egg Fried Rice
- Lemon Garlic Chicken Thighs
- Quick Turkey Meatball Soup
- Spicy Sausage and Peppers
- Tuna Salad Lettuce Wraps
- 20-Minute Chickpea Curry
- Quick Chicken and Veggie Stir-Fry
- Shrimp and Veggie Skewers
- One-Pot Mexican Rice

- Quick Veggie Tacos with Avocado
- Sweet and Sour Pork Stir-Fry
- Beef and Spinach Frittata
- 15-Minute Pesto Pasta
- Easy Beef Tacos
- One-Skillet Sausage and Potatoes
- Quick Garlic Butter Chicken Bites
- 20-Minute Chicken Marsala
- Quick Veggie and Cheese Quesadillas
- Spicy Ramen Stir-Fry
- Pita Pizza with Veggies
- 30-Minute Shrimp Scampi
- Quick Sweet Potato Hash
- Easy Pesto Chicken

Quick Stir-Fry Beef and Veggies

Ingredients:

- 1 lb beef sirloin or flank steak, thinly sliced
- 2 tbsp soy sauce
- 1 tbsp hoisin sauce
- 1 tbsp oyster sauce
- 1 tbsp sesame oil
- 1 bell pepper, sliced
- 1 carrot, thinly sliced
- 1/2 onion, sliced
- 2 cloves garlic, minced
- 1 tbsp ginger, minced
- 2 tbsp vegetable oil
- 1 tbsp sesame seeds (optional)

Instructions:

1. In a small bowl, mix soy sauce, hoisin sauce, oyster sauce, and sesame oil.
2. Heat vegetable oil in a large pan or wok over medium-high heat.
3. Add the beef and stir-fry for 2-3 minutes until browned, then set aside.
4. In the same pan, add garlic, ginger, and vegetables. Stir-fry for 4-5 minutes until tender-crisp.

5. Add the beef back into the pan and pour the sauce over everything. Stir to coat and cook for another 2-3 minutes.

6. Garnish with sesame seeds and serve with rice or noodles.

15-Minute Garlic Shrimp Pasta

Ingredients:

- 8 oz pasta (spaghetti, linguine, or your choice)
- 1 lb shrimp, peeled and deveined
- 4 cloves garlic, minced
- 1 tbsp olive oil
- 1 tbsp butter
- 1/2 tsp red pepper flakes
- 1/4 cup grated Parmesan cheese
- Salt and pepper to taste
- Fresh parsley, chopped for garnish

Instructions:

1. Cook the pasta according to package instructions, then drain and set aside.
2. While the pasta cooks, heat olive oil and butter in a large pan over medium heat.
3. Add garlic and red pepper flakes, cooking for 1-2 minutes until fragrant.
4. Add the shrimp and cook for 3-4 minutes until pink and cooked through.
5. Toss in the cooked pasta, season with salt and pepper, and sprinkle with Parmesan cheese.
6. Garnish with fresh parsley and serve.

Easy One-Pan Chicken Fajitas

Ingredients:

- 1 lb chicken breast, thinly sliced
- 1 bell pepper, sliced
- 1 onion, sliced
- 2 tbsp olive oil
- 1 tbsp chili powder
- 1 tsp cumin
- 1 tsp paprika
- Salt and pepper to taste
- Tortillas, for serving
- Fresh cilantro, chopped for garnish
- Lime wedges, for serving

Instructions:

1. Preheat oven to 400°F (200°C).
2. Toss the chicken, bell pepper, and onion in olive oil and season with chili powder, cumin, paprika, salt, and pepper.
3. Spread the mixture evenly on a baking sheet.
4. Bake for 20-25 minutes, stirring halfway, until the chicken is cooked through.

5. Serve with tortillas, garnish with fresh cilantro, and squeeze lime juice over the top.

Spicy Veggie Tacos

Ingredients:

- 1 can black beans, drained and rinsed
- 1 cup corn kernels (frozen or canned)
- 1 bell pepper, diced
- 1 zucchini, diced
- 1 tbsp olive oil
- 1 tsp chili powder
- 1/2 tsp cumin
- Salt and pepper to taste
- Small tortillas
- Toppings: avocado, salsa, sour cream, cilantro, lime

Instructions:

1. Heat olive oil in a skillet over medium heat.
2. Add the bell pepper, zucchini, and corn. Cook for 5-7 minutes until softened.
3. Stir in black beans, chili powder, cumin, salt, and pepper. Cook for another 2-3 minutes.
4. Warm the tortillas in a dry skillet.
5. Fill the tortillas with the veggie mixture and top with avocado, salsa, sour cream, cilantro, and lime juice.

One-Pot Garlic Parmesan Pasta

Ingredients:

- 8 oz pasta (your choice)
- 4 cups chicken broth
- 3 cloves garlic, minced
- 1 cup heavy cream
- 1 cup grated Parmesan cheese
- 2 tbsp butter
- Salt and pepper to taste

Instructions:

1. In a large pot, combine pasta, chicken broth, and garlic. Bring to a boil over medium-high heat.
2. Reduce heat to low and simmer, uncovered, for 10-12 minutes, stirring occasionally until the pasta is tender and the liquid is mostly absorbed.
3. Stir in butter, heavy cream, and Parmesan cheese. Season with salt and pepper.
4. Cook for another 2-3 minutes, until creamy and smooth. Serve warm.

Chicken Caesar Salad Wraps

Ingredients:

- 2 cooked chicken breasts, sliced
- 4 large flour tortillas
- 2 cups Romaine lettuce, chopped
- 1/4 cup grated Parmesan cheese
- 1/4 cup Caesar dressing
- Salt and pepper to taste

Instructions:

1. In a bowl, toss the chicken, lettuce, Parmesan cheese, and Caesar dressing until well coated.
2. Season with salt and pepper to taste.
3. Divide the mixture among the tortillas and wrap tightly.
4. Slice and serve.

Quick Veggie and Bean Chili

Ingredients:

- 1 can kidney beans, drained and rinsed
- 1 can black beans, drained and rinsed
- 1 can diced tomatoes (14.5 oz)
- 1 cup corn kernels (frozen or canned)
- 1 bell pepper, chopped
- 1 onion, chopped
- 2 cloves garlic, minced
- 2 tsp chili powder
- 1 tsp cumin
- Salt and pepper to taste

Instructions:

1. In a large pot, sauté the onion, bell pepper, and garlic over medium heat for 3-4 minutes.
2. Add the beans, tomatoes, corn, chili powder, cumin, salt, and pepper.
3. Bring to a simmer and cook for 10-15 minutes, stirring occasionally.
4. Serve with toppings like sour cream, cheese, and cilantro.

20-Minute Chicken Alfredo

Ingredients:

- 1 lb chicken breast, diced
- 8 oz pasta (fettuccine or your choice)
- 2 tbsp olive oil
- 3/4 cup heavy cream
- 1 cup grated Parmesan cheese
- 1/2 tsp garlic powder
- Salt and pepper to taste

Instructions:

1. Cook the pasta according to package instructions, then drain and set aside.
2. Heat olive oil in a large pan over medium heat. Add diced chicken and cook for 5-6 minutes until browned and cooked through.
3. Stir in heavy cream, garlic powder, and Parmesan cheese. Cook for another 2-3 minutes until the sauce thickens.
4. Toss the cooked pasta into the sauce and mix well. Season with salt and pepper.
5. Serve with extra Parmesan cheese.

Easy Beef Stir-Fry with Broccoli

Ingredients:

- 1 lb beef (sirloin or flank steak), thinly sliced
- 2 cups broccoli florets
- 2 tbsp soy sauce
- 1 tbsp oyster sauce
- 1 tbsp sesame oil
- 1 tbsp vegetable oil
- 2 cloves garlic, minced
- 1/2 tsp ginger, minced

Instructions:

1. Heat vegetable oil in a wok or large skillet over medium-high heat.
2. Add the beef and cook for 3-4 minutes until browned. Remove and set aside.
3. In the same pan, add garlic, ginger, and broccoli. Stir-fry for 4-5 minutes until tender-crisp.
4. Add the beef back to the pan and stir in soy sauce, oyster sauce, and sesame oil.
5. Cook for another 2-3 minutes, then serve.

Quick Teriyaki Chicken Skewers

Ingredients:

- 1 lb chicken breast, cut into cubes
- 1/4 cup soy sauce
- 2 tbsp honey
- 1 tbsp rice vinegar
- 1 tsp sesame oil
- 1 clove garlic, minced
- 1 tbsp ginger, minced
- 1 tbsp sesame seeds (optional)

Instructions:

1. In a bowl, mix soy sauce, honey, rice vinegar, sesame oil, garlic, and ginger.
2. Add chicken cubes and marinate for 10-15 minutes.
3. Preheat the grill or oven to medium-high heat. Thread chicken onto skewers.
4. Grill or bake for 8-10 minutes, flipping halfway through, until cooked through.
5. Garnish with sesame seeds and serve.

One-Pot Beef Stroganoff

Ingredients:

- 1 lb ground beef
- 1 onion, chopped
- 3 cloves garlic, minced
- 2 tbsp flour
- 3 cups beef broth
- 1 cup sour cream
- 8 oz egg noodles
- 2 tbsp butter
- Salt and pepper to taste

Instructions:

1. In a large pot, brown the ground beef over medium heat. Remove excess fat.
2. Add onion and garlic, cooking for 2-3 minutes until softened.
3. Stir in flour and cook for 1 minute.
4. Add beef broth, bring to a simmer, then stir in egg noodles.
5. Cook for 8-10 minutes until noodles are tender and the liquid thickens.
6. Stir in sour cream and butter, season with salt and pepper.
7. Serve warm.

Garlic Butter Shrimp and Asparagus

Ingredients:

- 1 lb shrimp, peeled and deveined
- 1 bunch asparagus, trimmed and cut into 2-inch pieces
- 4 cloves garlic, minced
- 2 tbsp butter
- 1 tbsp olive oil
- Salt and pepper to taste
- Fresh lemon wedges, for garnish

Instructions:

1. Heat olive oil and butter in a large skillet over medium-high heat.
2. Add garlic and cook for 1 minute until fragrant.
3. Add the shrimp and asparagus. Cook for 3-4 minutes until shrimp are pink and cooked through, and asparagus is tender.
4. Season with salt and pepper to taste. Serve with a squeeze of fresh lemon.

15-Minute Veggie Fried Rice

Ingredients:

- 2 cups cooked rice (preferably cold)
- 1 cup mixed veggies (carrots, peas, corn)
- 2 tbsp soy sauce
- 1 tbsp sesame oil
- 2 eggs, lightly beaten
- 2 cloves garlic, minced
- 1/2 onion, chopped
- 2 green onions, sliced

Instructions:

1. Heat sesame oil in a large pan over medium heat.
2. Add garlic and onion, cooking for 2 minutes until fragrant.
3. Push the veggies and onions to one side of the pan. Scramble the eggs in the empty space, then mix everything together.
4. Add the rice, soy sauce, and green onions. Stir-fry for 3-5 minutes until everything is heated through.
5. Serve immediately.

Quick BBQ Chicken Quesadillas

Ingredients:

- 2 cooked chicken breasts, shredded
- 1/2 cup BBQ sauce
- 1 cup shredded cheese (cheddar, mozzarella, or a blend)
- 4 flour tortillas
- 1/2 cup red onion, sliced
- 1 tbsp olive oil

Instructions:

1. Preheat a skillet over medium heat. Brush one side of each tortilla with olive oil.
2. On the non-oiled side, spread BBQ sauce, then add shredded chicken, cheese, and red onions.
3. Place a tortilla in the skillet, oiled side down. Cook for 2-3 minutes until golden and crispy, then flip and cook the other side.
4. Slice into wedges and serve.

30-Minute Salmon and Veggie Packets

Ingredients:

- 4 salmon fillets
- 2 cups mixed veggies (zucchini, bell pepper, cherry tomatoes, etc.)
- 2 tbsp olive oil
- 1 tbsp lemon juice
- 1 tsp garlic powder
- Salt and pepper to taste
- Aluminum foil

Instructions:

1. Preheat oven to 400°F (200°C).
2. Cut 4 large pieces of aluminum foil. Place a salmon fillet in the center of each.
3. Drizzle with olive oil, lemon juice, garlic powder, salt, and pepper. Top with mixed veggies.
4. Fold the foil around the salmon and veggies to create a packet. Place on a baking sheet.
5. Bake for 15-20 minutes until the salmon is cooked through and flakes easily with a fork.

One-Skillet Lemon Herb Chicken

Ingredients:

- 4 boneless chicken breasts
- 1 tbsp olive oil
- 1 tbsp lemon zest
- 1 tbsp lemon juice
- 2 cloves garlic, minced
- 1 tsp dried thyme
- Salt and pepper to taste

Instructions:

1. Heat olive oil in a large skillet over medium heat.
2. Season the chicken breasts with lemon zest, lemon juice, garlic, thyme, salt, and pepper.
3. Cook the chicken for 6-7 minutes on each side until golden and cooked through.
4. Serve with extra lemon wedges and fresh herbs.

Fast Chicken Parmesan

Ingredients:

- 2 chicken breasts, breaded and cooked
- 1 cup marinara sauce
- 1 cup shredded mozzarella cheese
- 1/4 cup grated Parmesan cheese
- 1 tbsp olive oil
- Fresh basil for garnish

Instructions:

1. Preheat oven to 400°F (200°C).
2. Heat olive oil in a skillet over medium heat. Add the breaded chicken and cook for 2-3 minutes on each side until golden.
3. Top each chicken breast with marinara sauce and cheese. Place the skillet in the oven and bake for 5-7 minutes until the cheese is melted.
4. Garnish with fresh basil and serve with pasta or a side salad.

20-Minute Fish Tacos

Ingredients:

- 1 lb white fish fillets (cod, tilapia, or your choice)
- 1 tsp chili powder
- 1/2 tsp cumin
- 1 tbsp olive oil
- 1/2 cup shredded cabbage
- 1/4 cup sour cream
- 1 tbsp lime juice
- Corn tortillas
- Fresh cilantro, for garnish

Instructions:

1. Heat olive oil in a skillet over medium heat.
2. Season the fish with chili powder, cumin, salt, and pepper. Cook for 3-4 minutes on each side until the fish is cooked through.
3. Mix sour cream and lime juice in a small bowl.
4. Warm the tortillas in a dry skillet. Fill each tortilla with fish, cabbage, and a drizzle of sour cream sauce.
5. Garnish with fresh cilantro and serve.

Spaghetti Aglio e Olio

Ingredients:

- 8 oz spaghetti
- 4 cloves garlic, sliced
- 1/4 cup olive oil
- 1/4 tsp red pepper flakes
- Fresh parsley, chopped for garnish
- Salt to taste

Instructions:

1. Cook the spaghetti according to package instructions, then drain and reserve 1/2 cup of pasta water.
2. Heat olive oil in a skillet over medium heat. Add the garlic and red pepper flakes. Cook for 1-2 minutes until fragrant.
3. Add the cooked spaghetti to the skillet, tossing to coat in the garlic oil. Add reserved pasta water if needed to loosen the sauce.
4. Season with salt and garnish with fresh parsley.

One-Pot Spaghetti Bolognese

Ingredients:

- 1 lb ground beef or turkey
- 1 onion, chopped
- 2 cloves garlic, minced
- 1 can crushed tomatoes (14.5 oz)
- 2 cups beef broth
- 8 oz spaghetti
- 1 tbsp olive oil
- 1 tsp dried oregano
- Salt and pepper to taste
- Fresh basil for garnish

Instructions:

1. Heat olive oil in a large pot over medium heat. Add ground beef and cook until browned.
2. Add onion and garlic, cooking for 3 minutes until softened.
3. Stir in crushed tomatoes, beef broth, oregano, salt, and pepper. Bring to a simmer.
4. Add the spaghetti and cook for 10-12 minutes until tender, stirring occasionally.
5. Garnish with fresh basil and serve.

Veggie and Hummus Pita Pockets

Ingredients:

- 4 whole wheat pita pockets
- 1 cup hummus
- 1 cucumber, sliced
- 1 tomato, sliced
- 1/4 red onion, thinly sliced
- Fresh spinach or lettuce
- Feta cheese (optional)

Instructions:

1. Cut the pitas in half to form pockets.
2. Spread a generous amount of hummus inside each pita.
3. Stuff with cucumber, tomato, onion, spinach, and feta cheese if using.
4. Serve immediately or refrigerate for a quick meal later.

Grilled Cheese and Tomato Soup

Ingredients:

- 4 slices of bread
- 4 slices of cheddar cheese
- 2 tbsp butter
- 2 cups tomato soup (store-bought or homemade)
- Salt and pepper to taste

Instructions:

1. Butter one side of each slice of bread. Place cheese between the slices, buttered side out.
2. Heat a skillet over medium heat and grill the sandwiches until golden brown on both sides, about 3-4 minutes per side.
3. While the sandwiches are grilling, heat the tomato soup in a pot over medium heat.
4. Serve the grilled cheese with a bowl of hot tomato soup.

30-Minute Beef and Broccoli

Ingredients:

- 1 lb beef sirloin or flank steak, thinly sliced
- 2 cups broccoli florets
- 2 tbsp soy sauce
- 2 tbsp oyster sauce
- 1 tbsp cornstarch
- 2 cloves garlic, minced
- 1 tbsp sesame oil
- 1 tbsp vegetable oil

Instructions:

1. Mix soy sauce, oyster sauce, and cornstarch in a bowl. Add the beef and toss to coat.
2. Heat vegetable oil in a skillet over medium-high heat. Add the beef and cook for 3-4 minutes until browned. Remove from the skillet.
3. Add sesame oil to the skillet, then add the garlic and cook for 30 seconds. Add the broccoli and cook for 2-3 minutes until tender.
4. Return the beef to the skillet and toss with the broccoli. Cook for another 2 minutes to combine.
5. Serve with rice or noodles.

Quick Sweet and Sour Chicken

Ingredients:

- 1 lb chicken breast, cut into bite-sized pieces
- 1 cup bell peppers, sliced
- 1/2 cup pineapple chunks
- 1/4 cup sweet and sour sauce
- 1 tbsp soy sauce
- 1 tbsp vegetable oil

Instructions:

1. Heat vegetable oil in a skillet over medium heat. Add the chicken and cook until browned and cooked through, about 5-7 minutes.
2. Add the bell peppers and pineapple, cooking for 2 minutes.
3. Stir in sweet and sour sauce and soy sauce. Cook for another 2 minutes until heated through.
4. Serve with rice or noodles.

Sheet Pan Chicken and Veggies

Ingredients:

- 4 boneless chicken thighs or breasts
- 1 cup carrots, sliced
- 1 cup zucchini, sliced
- 1 tbsp olive oil
- 1 tsp garlic powder
- 1 tsp dried thyme
- Salt and pepper to taste

Instructions:

1. Preheat oven to 400°F (200°C).
2. Place the chicken and vegetables on a baking sheet. Drizzle with olive oil and season with garlic powder, thyme, salt, and pepper.
3. Roast for 20-25 minutes, flipping the chicken halfway through, until the chicken is cooked through and the veggies are tender.
4. Serve immediately.

Quick Baked Ziti

Ingredients:

- 8 oz ziti pasta
- 2 cups marinara sauce
- 1 1/2 cups ricotta cheese
- 1 1/2 cups shredded mozzarella cheese
- 1/2 cup grated Parmesan cheese

Instructions:

1. Preheat oven to 375°F (190°C). Cook the ziti according to package instructions, then drain.
2. Mix the cooked pasta with marinara sauce, ricotta, and half of the mozzarella cheese. Pour into a greased baking dish.
3. Top with remaining mozzarella and Parmesan cheese.
4. Bake for 15-20 minutes until the cheese is melted and bubbly. Serve hot.

Teriyaki Beef Bowls

Ingredients:

- 1 lb beef sirloin, thinly sliced
- 1 cup teriyaki sauce
- 1 cup cooked rice
- 1/2 cup sliced green onions
- 1/4 cup sesame seeds

Instructions:

1. Heat a skillet over medium-high heat. Add the beef and cook for 3-4 minutes until browned.
2. Pour in the teriyaki sauce and simmer for 5-7 minutes, allowing the sauce to thicken.
3. Serve the beef over a bowl of rice and top with green onions and sesame seeds.

15-Minute Egg Fried Rice

Ingredients:

- 2 cups cooked rice (preferably cold)
- 2 eggs, scrambled
- 1 cup mixed veggies (peas, carrots, corn)
- 2 tbsp soy sauce
- 1 tbsp sesame oil
- 1/4 cup green onions, chopped

Instructions:

1. Heat sesame oil in a pan over medium-high heat. Add the scrambled eggs and cook for 2 minutes, then remove from the pan.
2. Add the mixed veggies to the pan and cook for 2 minutes. Add the rice and soy sauce, stirring to combine.
3. Return the eggs to the pan, mix everything together, and cook for another 2-3 minutes. Top with green onions and serve.

Lemon Garlic Chicken Thighs

Ingredients:

- 4 chicken thighs
- 2 tbsp olive oil
- 4 cloves garlic, minced
- 1 lemon, zested and juiced
- Salt and pepper to taste

Instructions:

1. Preheat oven to 400°F (200°C).
2. Heat olive oil in a skillet over medium-high heat. Season the chicken thighs with salt and pepper.
3. Cook the chicken for 4-5 minutes on each side until browned.
4. Add garlic and lemon zest, cooking for another 1-2 minutes until fragrant. Squeeze in lemon juice and transfer the skillet to the oven.
5. Roast for 15-20 minutes until the chicken is cooked through. Serve with your favorite side.

Quick Turkey Meatball Soup

Ingredients:

- 1 lb ground turkey
- 1/2 cup breadcrumbs
- 1 egg
- 4 cups chicken broth
- 1 cup spinach
- 1/2 cup carrots, chopped
- 1/4 cup Parmesan cheese
- Salt and pepper to taste

Instructions:

1. In a bowl, combine ground turkey, breadcrumbs, egg, Parmesan, salt, and pepper. Form into small meatballs.
2. In a large pot, bring chicken broth to a boil. Add the meatballs and cook for 5-7 minutes until they float.
3. Add the carrots and spinach, cooking for another 5 minutes until tender. Serve hot.

Spicy Sausage and Peppers

Ingredients:

- 4 spicy Italian sausages
- 2 bell peppers, sliced
- 1 onion, sliced
- 1 tbsp olive oil
- 1 tsp red pepper flakes
- Salt and pepper to taste

Instructions:

1. Heat olive oil in a skillet over medium heat. Add the sausages and cook until browned on all sides, about 8-10 minutes. Remove from the pan and slice.
2. In the same pan, add the bell peppers, onion, and red pepper flakes. Cook for 5-7 minutes until softened.
3. Add the sausage slices back into the pan and cook for another 2-3 minutes. Serve immediately.

Tuna Salad Lettuce Wraps

Ingredients:

- 1 can tuna, drained
- 1/4 cup mayonnaise
- 1 tbsp Dijon mustard
- 1 tbsp lemon juice
- 1/4 cup diced celery
- Salt and pepper to taste
- 8-10 large lettuce leaves (such as Romaine)

Instructions:

1. In a bowl, mix together the tuna, mayonnaise, Dijon mustard, lemon juice, celery, salt, and pepper.
2. Spoon the tuna salad into the center of each lettuce leaf.
3. Roll the lettuce around the filling and enjoy!

20-Minute Chickpea Curry

Ingredients:

- 1 can chickpeas, drained and rinsed
- 1 can diced tomatoes
- 1/2 cup coconut milk
- 1 onion, diced
- 2 cloves garlic, minced
- 1 tbsp curry powder
- 1/2 tsp turmeric
- 1/2 tsp cumin
- Salt and pepper to taste
- Fresh cilantro for garnish

Instructions:

1. In a large skillet, heat a little oil over medium heat. Add the onion and garlic, and cook until softened, about 3-4 minutes.
2. Add the curry powder, turmeric, and cumin, and cook for another minute.
3. Add the chickpeas, diced tomatoes, and coconut milk. Stir to combine, and let the curry simmer for 10 minutes.
4. Season with salt and pepper, and serve with rice or naan. Garnish with cilantro.

Quick Chicken and Veggie Stir-Fry

Ingredients:

- 2 chicken breasts, thinly sliced
- 1 cup mixed vegetables (broccoli, carrots, bell peppers, etc.)
- 2 tbsp soy sauce
- 1 tbsp sesame oil
- 1 tbsp honey
- 1 tsp ginger, minced
- 1 tsp garlic, minced
- 1 tbsp cornstarch (optional, for thickening)

Instructions:

1. Heat sesame oil in a skillet over medium-high heat. Add the chicken and cook for 5-6 minutes, until browned.
2. Add the garlic and ginger, and cook for another 1 minute.
3. Add the mixed vegetables, soy sauce, and honey. Stir well and cook for 5 minutes, until the vegetables are tender.
4. If you'd like a thicker sauce, mix the cornstarch with a little water and add it to the pan, cooking for another 2 minutes.
5. Serve over rice or noodles.

Shrimp and Veggie Skewers

Ingredients:

- 1 lb shrimp, peeled and deveined
- 1 zucchini, sliced
- 1 red bell pepper, sliced
- 1/2 red onion, cut into chunks
- 2 tbsp olive oil
- 1 tsp garlic powder
- 1 tsp paprika
- Salt and pepper to taste

Instructions:

1. Preheat grill or grill pan to medium-high heat.
2. Thread shrimp and veggies onto skewers.
3. Drizzle with olive oil, and season with garlic powder, paprika, salt, and pepper.
4. Grill the skewers for 3-4 minutes per side, until the shrimp are pink and cooked through.
5. Serve with rice or a side salad.

One-Pot Mexican Rice

Ingredients:

- 1 cup long-grain rice
- 1 can diced tomatoes
- 1 cup chicken broth
- 1/2 cup diced onions
- 1/2 cup bell peppers, diced
- 1 tbsp chili powder
- 1/2 tsp cumin
- Salt and pepper to taste

Instructions:

1. In a large pot, heat a little oil over medium heat. Add the onions and bell peppers and cook for 3-4 minutes until softened.
2. Add the rice and cook for 1-2 minutes, stirring frequently.
3. Stir in the diced tomatoes, chicken broth, chili powder, cumin, salt, and pepper. Bring to a simmer.
4. Cover the pot, reduce the heat to low, and cook for 15-20 minutes, until the rice is tender and the liquid is absorbed.
5. Fluff with a fork and serve.

Quick Veggie Tacos with Avocado

Ingredients:

- 1 can black beans, drained and rinsed
- 1 cup corn kernels
- 1 tbsp olive oil
- 1 tsp chili powder
- 1/2 tsp cumin
- 1/4 tsp paprika
- Salt and pepper to taste
- 6 small tortillas
- 1 avocado, sliced
- Fresh cilantro for garnish
- Lime wedges for serving

Instructions:

1. In a skillet, heat olive oil over medium heat. Add the black beans, corn, chili powder, cumin, paprika, salt, and pepper.
2. Cook for 5-7 minutes, stirring occasionally until heated through.
3. Warm the tortillas, and then spoon the veggie mixture into each one.
4. Top with avocado slices, cilantro, and a squeeze of lime juice.

Sweet and Sour Pork Stir-Fry

Ingredients:

- 1 lb pork tenderloin, thinly sliced
- 1/2 cup pineapple chunks
- 1 bell pepper, sliced
- 1 onion, sliced
- 2 cloves garlic, minced
- 1/4 cup rice vinegar
- 3 tbsp soy sauce
- 2 tbsp brown sugar
- 1 tbsp cornstarch (optional, for thickening)

Instructions:

1. Heat a little oil in a skillet over medium-high heat. Add the pork and cook for 5-6 minutes, until browned.

2. Add the garlic, bell pepper, onion, and pineapple. Cook for another 3-4 minutes, until the vegetables are tender.

3. In a bowl, mix the rice vinegar, soy sauce, and brown sugar. Pour over the pork and veggies and cook for 2-3 minutes.

4. If you'd like a thicker sauce, mix the cornstarch with a little water and add it to the pan, cooking for another 2 minutes.

5. Serve over rice or noodles.

Beef and Spinach Frittata

Ingredients:

- 1 lb ground beef
- 1/2 cup spinach, chopped
- 8 eggs
- 1/2 cup shredded cheese (optional)
- Salt and pepper to taste
- 1 tbsp olive oil

Instructions:

1. Preheat the oven to 350°F (175°C).
2. In an oven-safe skillet, heat olive oil over medium heat. Add the ground beef and cook until browned, about 5-6 minutes.
3. Add the chopped spinach and cook until wilted, about 2 minutes.
4. In a bowl, whisk together the eggs, cheese, salt, and pepper. Pour over the beef and spinach mixture.
5. Transfer the skillet to the oven and bake for 15-20 minutes, until the eggs are set and lightly golden.
6. Serve warm.

15-Minute Pesto Pasta

Ingredients:

- 8 oz pasta of your choice
- 1/4 cup pesto sauce (store-bought or homemade)
- 1 tbsp olive oil
- 1 tbsp Parmesan cheese (optional)
- Salt and pepper to taste

Instructions:

1. Cook the pasta according to package instructions. Drain and set aside.
2. In the same pot, toss the pasta with pesto sauce and olive oil. Cook over low heat for 2-3 minutes.
3. Season with salt and pepper, and top with Parmesan cheese if desired.

Easy Beef Tacos

Ingredients:

- 1 lb ground beef
- 1 packet taco seasoning
- 1/4 cup water
- 6 taco shells
- 1 cup shredded lettuce
- 1/2 cup shredded cheese
- 1/2 cup salsa

Instructions:

1. In a skillet, cook the ground beef over medium-high heat until browned, about 5-7 minutes.
2. Add the taco seasoning and water, and cook for another 2-3 minutes until well combined.
3. Spoon the beef mixture into taco shells and top with lettuce, cheese, and salsa.

One-Skillet Sausage and Potatoes

Ingredients:

- 1 lb sausage (Italian, chicken, or your choice)
- 1 lb baby potatoes, halved or quartered
- 1 onion, sliced
- 2 cloves garlic, minced
- 1 tsp paprika
- 1/2 tsp thyme
- Salt and pepper to taste
- Olive oil for cooking

Instructions:

1. Heat olive oil in a large skillet over medium heat.
2. Add the sausage and cook until browned, about 5-6 minutes. Remove and set aside.
3. In the same skillet, add the potatoes and cook for about 8-10 minutes, stirring occasionally.
4. Add the onion and garlic, cooking for 2 minutes until softened.
5. Return the sausage to the skillet, add paprika, thyme, salt, and pepper, and cook for another 5-7 minutes until everything is fully cooked through.
6. Serve hot!

Quick Garlic Butter Chicken Bites

Ingredients:

- 2 chicken breasts, cut into bite-sized pieces
- 2 tbsp butter
- 3 cloves garlic, minced
- 1 tsp Italian seasoning
- Salt and pepper to taste
- Fresh parsley for garnish (optional)

Instructions:

1. In a skillet, melt the butter over medium heat.
2. Add the chicken and cook until browned on all sides, about 5-7 minutes.
3. Add the garlic and Italian seasoning, and cook for another 1-2 minutes until fragrant.
4. Season with salt and pepper, and garnish with fresh parsley if desired.
5. Serve with rice or veggies!

20-Minute Chicken Marsala

Ingredients:

- 2 chicken breasts, pounded thin
- 1 cup mushrooms, sliced
- 1/2 cup Marsala wine
- 1/2 cup chicken broth
- 2 tbsp butter
- 1 tbsp olive oil
- Salt and pepper to taste

Instructions:

1. In a large skillet, heat olive oil over medium heat. Cook the chicken for 4-5 minutes on each side until golden brown and cooked through. Remove from the skillet.

2. In the same skillet, add butter and mushrooms. Cook for 3-4 minutes until softened.

3. Add the Marsala wine and chicken broth, bringing it to a simmer. Let the sauce reduce for 2-3 minutes.

4. Return the chicken to the skillet, simmer for an additional 2-3 minutes, and season with salt and pepper.

5. Serve with mashed potatoes or pasta.

Quick Veggie and Cheese Quesadillas

Ingredients:

- 4 flour tortillas
- 1 cup shredded cheese (cheddar, Monterey Jack, etc.)
- 1 cup mixed veggies (bell peppers, onions, spinach, etc.)
- 1 tbsp olive oil
- Salt and pepper to taste

Instructions:

1. Heat olive oil in a skillet over medium heat. Add the mixed veggies and sauté until softened, about 4-5 minutes.
2. Place a tortilla in the skillet and sprinkle with cheese and sautéed veggies. Top with another tortilla.
3. Cook for 2-3 minutes per side, pressing down gently, until the cheese is melted and the tortilla is golden.
4. Slice and serve with salsa and sour cream.

Spicy Ramen Stir-Fry

Ingredients:

- 2 packs instant ramen (discard the seasoning packet)
- 1/2 cup mixed veggies (carrots, bell peppers, peas, etc.)
- 2 tbsp soy sauce
- 1 tbsp sriracha or hot sauce
- 1 tbsp sesame oil
- 1 tbsp olive oil
- 1 green onion, chopped (optional)

Instructions:

1. Cook the ramen according to package instructions, then drain and set aside.
2. In a large skillet or wok, heat olive oil and sesame oil over medium-high heat. Add the veggies and sauté for 3-4 minutes.
3. Add the cooked ramen, soy sauce, and sriracha, and toss to combine. Cook for another 2-3 minutes, allowing the noodles to get crispy in some spots.
4. Top with green onions and serve hot.

Pita Pizza with Veggies

Ingredients:

- 2 whole-wheat pita breads
- 1/2 cup tomato sauce
- 1 cup shredded mozzarella cheese
- 1/2 cup bell peppers, sliced
- 1/4 cup red onion, thinly sliced
- 1/4 cup olives, sliced
- 1 tsp dried oregano
- Olive oil for brushing

Instructions:

1. Preheat the oven to 400°F (200°C).
2. Place the pita breads on a baking sheet and brush lightly with olive oil.
3. Spread a thin layer of tomato sauce on each pita, then sprinkle with mozzarella cheese.
4. Add the bell peppers, onions, olives, and oregano.
5. Bake for 8-10 minutes, or until the cheese is melted and the crust is golden.
6. Slice and serve hot.

30-Minute Shrimp Scampi

Ingredients:

- 1 lb shrimp, peeled and deveined
- 8 oz pasta (linguine, spaghetti, etc.)
- 4 tbsp butter
- 4 cloves garlic, minced
- 1/2 cup white wine or chicken broth
- 1/4 cup fresh parsley, chopped
- 1 tbsp lemon juice
- Salt and pepper to taste

Instructions:

1. Cook the pasta according to package instructions, then drain and set aside.
2. In a large skillet, melt butter over medium heat. Add garlic and cook for 1-2 minutes until fragrant.
3. Add the shrimp to the skillet and cook for 3-4 minutes, until pink and cooked through.
4. Add white wine or broth, lemon juice, and cooked pasta. Toss to combine, and cook for another 2 minutes.
5. Sprinkle with parsley and season with salt and pepper. Serve hot.

Quick Sweet Potato Hash

Ingredients:

- 2 medium sweet potatoes, peeled and diced
- 1 bell pepper, diced
- 1 onion, diced
- 1 tsp paprika
- 1/2 tsp garlic powder
- Salt and pepper to taste
- Olive oil for cooking
- 1/2 cup cooked bacon or sausage (optional)

Instructions:

1. Heat olive oil in a skillet over medium heat. Add the diced sweet potatoes and cook for 10-12 minutes, stirring occasionally, until tender.
2. Add the bell pepper, onion, paprika, garlic powder, salt, and pepper. Cook for another 5 minutes until the veggies are soft.
3. Optionally, stir in cooked bacon or sausage.
4. Serve with eggs or on its own!

Easy Pesto Chicken

Ingredients:

- 2 chicken breasts
- 1/4 cup pesto sauce (store-bought or homemade)
- 1 tbsp olive oil
- Salt and pepper to taste
- 1/4 cup shredded mozzarella cheese (optional)

Instructions:

1. Preheat the oven to 375°F (190°C).
2. Season the chicken breasts with salt and pepper.
3. Heat olive oil in a skillet over medium heat. Sear the chicken breasts for 3-4 minutes on each side.
4. Transfer the chicken to a baking dish, and spread pesto sauce over each piece.
5. Bake for 20-25 minutes, until the chicken is cooked through. Optionally, sprinkle with mozzarella cheese during the last 5 minutes of baking.
6. Serve with pasta or vegetables!